The

Victory

Walk

Victoria Riollano

ISBN: 1976387116
ISBN-13: 978-1976387111

DEDICATION

This book is dedicated in loving memory of "Ray" Riollano, a great man who was the gentle peace in the midst of storms and gave hope to the hurting.

CONTENTS

ACKNOWLEDGMENTS

I would like to give my humble thanks to everyone who has assisted me in the creation of this work. First, I would like to thank the Lord for the opportunity to minister to His people through words. It is an honor that I do not take for granted. I would like to thank my husband, Joseph Riollano, for always encouraging me to follow my God-given passion and providing me the time to do so amid our busy lives. Thank you, Joseph, for being a man of honor, respect, and wisdom that our children and I can look up to.

A major thanks to my mother and step-father, Angela and Reginald Benford, who never gave up on praying and believing for their daughter to live up to God's plans. I also want to give a special honor to Bishop Eddie Lee Stevens and Nancy Mae Stevens for being grandparents who were willing to stand in the gap and pray for me, by name daily. I am proud to say I have a praying grandmother. To all my other family members, whether by blood or marriage, thank you for supporting me thus far in all my endeavors.

Additionally, thank you to the Christian leaders and friends that are in my life. The prayers, last minute babysitting, and comfort needed as a busy mom and military spouse have been more than anyone can ask for. Thank you Hawani Tessema for assisting me in editing.

Lastly, I would like to thank my children Trinity, Joseph, Christian, Isaiah, David, and our newest princess on the way. You have each taught me how to love like Christ and view life from the Father's perspective. You have taught me that even the smallest victory is still a victory! I am forever grateful.

INTRODUCTION

Great news! You can live a life of victory! Victory is not subtle. In fact, it is a violent proclamation that I can win against all odds! The reality is that most people will live a life of defeat because they are unaware that the mundane, lackluster life does not belong to those who have accepted Christ!

In fact, Christ says that He came to give you life, and life more abundantly! The abundant life or full life is the victorious life! All we have to do is accept this life that Christ gives us and walk in it! It's time to walk in victory from this day forward.

The 21-Day Journey

Most psychologists agree that it takes 21 days to break a habit! These next 21 days have been designed to help you break the habit of a defeated life! The first seven days will focus on victory, itself. What is victory? How can I get it? The next seven days will point out victory blockers in your everyday life such as shame, unforgiveness, and fear! There are many more but let's start there. Finally, the last week is all about how to "walk the walk" and "talk the talk". It's not good enough to learn about victory, yet have no tools to move forward! I am privileged that you are using this book to start or continue your journey! Your victory walk will impact you and your generations to come! I pray that every weapon the enemy has used to defeat you in the past will be abolished in this time together! Whether you are a new Christian or one who has followed Christ for decades, we can all learn more on how to have a victorious life.

The goal of this entire devotional is to transition you from a mindset of defeat to one of victory. Take notes and reread the book more than once! I believe God is going to meet you and speak new revelation of His love and plan for you over the next 21 days!

If you can conquer the battle of the mind, it will be much easier to start walking into your victory! However, it would be unreasonable to think you will learn everything there is to know about victory in just 21 days. There are many aspects of what it means to walk victoriously in Christ. The goal is to unravel layer by layer what has been blocking you from your best life. Stick with the 21-day journey, reflect on the verses presented, answer the questions honestly, and seek the Lord. When you seek Him, He will answer. His answers will always be for your good!

Let's strap on our combat boots and start the victory walk!

PART 1

Victory Defined

1. *the overcoming of an enemy or antagonist, achievement of mastery or success in a struggle or endeavor against odds or difficulties*

2. *Success concerning warfare, where one's enemy is conquered*

Day One

What is Victory?

Recently, I asked a group of peers a question.

What is victory?

Many used the word "winning" as the ultimate determining factor of victory. Some instantly thought of their favorite sports team. While others, however, responded with a Christian phrase like "Jesus on the cross." In our society, victory can be equated with the word success. No matter what your description of victory is, we can all agree that we want it. Quite simply, the opposite of victory is to be defeated. There are few people you will meet that will desire a defeated life over a victorious life.

Victory is defined as the overcoming of an enemy or antagonist against all odds. In other words, victory is winning in a battle. This battle can be emotional, social, mental or physical. There are everyday victories like maintaining a fitness goal, scoring a new job, or learning to rest. Everyday victories can be handled easily in most cases. However, there are the bigger battles. Leaving a toxic relationship, overcoming anxiety, moving forward after a death, mending a broken relationship, or dropping an addiction are all bigger battles that we face. These are more intense circumstances and will take more effort and a strength that can only come from one place, a relationship with Christ.

Your relationship with Christ and how much you understand and utilize your God-given authority will make or break your ability to walk in victory. Having a great success here or there is a beautiful thing! However, those who love Christ should have a consistent life of victory. The victorious life requires you to view life from a different framework, or a new lens.

My favorite example of the victorious perspective can be found in the arena of pro-wrestling. Let me explain. Have you ever seen a WWE match? If you have, you understand that each match has already been rigged for the winner. Although the victor may take a few great hits and seem to be defeated, they will win! It is in the script! So, during each match they are not fighting FOR victory! Instead, they are well aware that they have ALREADY won, all they have to do is follow the moves! They have an attitude of victory every time, because they know the outcome.

We are not fighting FOR victory but FROM a place of

victory! In other words, you can have a stance of victory every time knowing that you can come through every situation against all odds.

Reflection Verse

Deuteronomy 20:4- For the LORD your God is the one who goes with you to fight for you against your enemies to give you victory.

Reflection Questions

1.) How would you define victory?

2.) Where did you gain your understanding of success?

3.) If you are honest with yourself, do you consider yourself victorious? Reflect on why you have your current perspective?

Day Two

The Pit of Defeat

Before we can go any deeper into victorious life, we must tackle the concept of the defeated life. Unfortunately, many Christians are living a life of defeat. One definition of defeat is to eliminate or deprive of something expected. In other words, the defeated life is one where you have come to expect "less than." It is a life that seems to always face one issue after another. It is a perspective as much as it is a lifestyle. Consider the questions below.

Do you find things never go right?

Do you feel defeated by your life, career, or family dynamics constantly?

Do you find that more people are against you than for you?

Have you come to expect the worst?

Do you tend to find the negative in most situations?

Do you have a list of regrets?

Do you have anxiety or fear about your overall life?

Do you often wonder why God is allowing so much to happen to you?

Do you find yourself anticipating when the next bad thing will happen?

If you answered yes to many of these questions, you may be living from a defeated perspective.

This perspective will keep you down and frustrated. This view of life will keep you in a place where you have no control over your emotions and the way you handle your everyday life. The reality is that many of us consider a depressed or sad person as one who is defeated. However, there are people all around you living this life. You may potentially be one of them. A frustrated mother who can't seem to get her children to listen, a man who has accepted he cannot find a job, a teen who has accepted failure in school, may all find themselves in a pit of defeat. Even if you think you have it all together, you may find yourself reverting to thoughts of defeat in your own life.

Many have found ourselves in this pit after years of

disappointment. Truthfully, the lives we have led thus far, the mistreatment from others, and low self-worth can leave us feeling defeated. It can be hard to accept that we are "victorious" when all we know is failure, and discouragement. It can be hard to accept this overarching theme of victory when we have yet to see it in our lives or those around us.

The reality is that our victory goes beyond what we can see with the natural eye. Even the person who appears to have the worst life, can have an attitude of victory. Consider people who are paralyzed, or have cancer, yet they dedicate their life to inspire others. They have decided to not allow their circumstances to determine their outlook.

Instead, they have shifted their outlook despite their circumstances.

With that in mind, you have a choice to make. Will you continue to live in the pit of defeat or will you choose to rise up and walk on the path of victory?

Reflection Verse

Matthew 11:28- Come to me, all who are heavy laden, and I will give you rest.

Reflection Questions

1.) Do you find your outlook on life is more defeated or victorious? Why or why not?

2.) What are some areas of your life where you feel like you are in a pit?

3.) In the past, when you have felt defeated, what gave you relief?

Day Three

Where Do We Find Our Victory?

We are now left with the daunting question. How does one live the "victorious" life? Where does this "victory" come from and how do we get it?

Quite simply, your victory comes from a relationship with Christ. For some, victory is equated with success, money, great friends, and winning. However, a victorious life has more to do with a mindset. A victorious life is one that is full of hope and grounded in truth. It is a life that recognizes that although things will get rough, we can always come through our toughest situations. Although many may appear to be victorious on the outside, the mindset of victory is one that is internal and should be the very heartbeat of every Christian.

Consider the inflatable punching bag which bounces back into place every time it gets knocked down. This is a great example of a mindset of victory. With every hit and every punch, it springs back into the upright position. Even more so, the harder you hit these toys, the quicker they bounce back up. It's very nature is to not be affected by the outside world. The wind or breath inside and the foundation allows it the ability to stand firm against every attack. The punching bag has victory from the inside-out.

So, what then is the breath that will keep us "bouncing back"? The Holy Spirit, the love of God, and His victory on the cross allows us the opportunity to never be deflated or defeated. Even if we do have moments of being attacked, and being down, we recognize that staying there is not an option.

1 Corinthians 15:57- But thanks be to God! He gives us the victory through our Lord Jesus Christ.

Romans 8:37- No, in all these things we are more than conquerors through him who loved us.

2 Corinthians 2:14- But thanks be to God, who always leads us as captives in Christ's triumphal procession and uses us to spread the aroma of the knowledge of him everywhere.

Philippians 4:13- I can do all this through him who gives me strength.

Jeremiah 29:11- For I know the plans I have for you," declares the Lord, "plans to prosper you and not to harm you, plans to give you hope and a future."

Our victory comes from knowing that God is on our side.

Our victory comes from knowing that He will fight against our enemies for us.

Our victory comes from knowing we can find our strength in Him.

Our victory comes from knowing that God will never leave us or forsake us.

Our victory comes from knowing that God has a plan for our lives.

Our victory comes from knowing that nothing can separate us from God's love.

Truthfully, ten chapters could be written on how we can come to terms with the idea that the victorious life is for us! The Bible is clear, victory belongs to all who belong to the Lord. If you have not accepted Christ in your life, NOW is the time to accept Him. If you are unsure whether you are a Christian, I ask that you pray this prayer below aloud and with your heart.

Dear Lord,

I invite you into my heart. I ask that you forgive me from all that I have done that has went against you. I confess that I am a sinner. Clean me from those things that have kept me separated from you. I repent of them all. I ask for you to be my Lord and my savior. I believe you died on the cross for my sins and rose again so that I can have a new life. Open my eyes so that I can clearly understand your word. In Jesus name.

If you have prayed that prayer today, I believe that everything that belongs to those who believe in Christ is now YOURS! There's no favoritism when it comes to God! Whether you have received Christ today or 15 years ago, every promise God declares for you from healing to victory, is yours.

Reflection Verse

John 3:16- For God so loved the world that he gave his one and only Son, that whoever believes in him shall not perish but have eternal life.

Reflection Questions

1.) John 3:16 says that God came to give us everlasting life. What does this mean to you? What implications does this have for you today?

2.) When considering the inflatable punching bag's ability to stand due to the air inside and its foundation, what do you feel is your foundation? The Word of God? Your desire to succeed?

3.) A list of phrases was provided above that explained where your victory comes from. Which two phrases spoke to you the most? Ask the Lord to give you two more phrases that describe the reason you can easily have an attitude of victory

Perspective in the Pit

The great news is that even if you are living a life of defeat you don't have to stay there. Truthfully, it's all about the power of perspective.

Recently, I was able to see the importance of perspective. Last year, my five-year-old received a letter from school. The letter explained that if he continued on his current trajectory, he would fail kindergarten. I began to panic and searched through his backpack to see how he had been performing this week in school. I must be honest, as a mother of five, I tend to not look through my children's backpacks as I should. However, as I dug through his things I found a small crumbled note. The note was telling how he failed the vision test two weeks prior. Within the next week, we had an appointment for the eye doctor. I learned that my son could not read lines that intersect. For instance, in the letter "t", he could only see the horizontal line or the vertical line. His eyes could not process both. Thus, reading would be virtually impossible without glasses. With the glasses, and weekly tutoring he was able to successfully catch up to his peers and learn to read.

My son did not have a disorder that limited his learning. Instead, he was in desperate need of a perspective change. He needed a lens to make things clearer for him to understand. He was in need of a new way of perceiving what was directly in front of him. The words in his school books didn't change; the way he filtered them changed. He was only able to learn to read because of the perspective shift he experienced. Furthermore, he would have remained unable to perceive properly had he not been willing to use the new glasses he was provided.

This brings us back to the pit. Many of us have found ourselves in a pit of fear of failure, disappointment, discouragement, regret, or even rejection. If you are to physically imagine yourself in a pit, the perspective is gloom. You would be able to see everyone above you living at a higher level. You would see them doing life and loving life. Meanwhile, you are the one that seems to go deeper and deeper into frustration. Your pit would leave you lonely, disregarded, and confused.

However, what if you decided to change your perspective during these moments? The reality is that while you are in the pit you can look around at the others who aren't in the pit with envy, OR you can look even higher straight to the sky. You can choose to have a perspective that focuses on man or one that focuses on God. Your perspective in the pit will determine your outcome, and the rate at which you come out. Even in the toughest times of your life, you can make a choice to choose your perspective

What if you chose from this day forward to shift your perspective?

Imagine you were fitted for new glasses, and the words on the lenses said the word "victory". This would entail that every situation would have to be seen from a different point of view. They could no longer be seen from a position of defeat or anticipated defeat. Instead, these new glasses would give you the ability to see all of life's issues through the lens of hope, victory, love and God's promises to you. Today, I am asking you to trade in your glasses for a new pair. The issue is so many of us have become accustomed to negative thinking and low expectations that this trade-in is almost impossible. The truth is, this perspective shift cannot fully come without complete surrender to Christ and trusting in His words for you. Within your own strength, it will be very difficult to change your perspective. Much like my son required the professional assistance of an eye doctor, you will also need the Lord to help you in this journey.

Reflection Verse

Romans 12:2 Do not conform to the pattern of this world, but be transformed by the renewing of your mind. Then you will be able to test and approve what God's will is—his good, pleasing and perfect will.

Reflection Questions

1.) Consider the last year of your life. How have you overcome when you have felt like you were in a pit?

2.) What are some areas of your life that you have a defeated perspective?

3.) What are some areas that you have a victorious perspective?

His Promises, Your Faith

This leads us to the next question. How can a person shift their perspective? Does one just wake up one day as a big ball of optimistic Jesus-loving energy? In my personal life, that would be a huge resounding NO! Although I have always seen myself as an optimistic person, this perspective of victory was one that came from a deeper non-superficial place. This perspective goes beyond seeing the best in every scenario, and is rooted in recognizing AND believing God's promises for your life.

1 John 5:4 says we will achieve victory through our faith. In other words, it will be our faith that takes us from being defeated to being victorious. Faith is having the ability to move past what your eyes can physically see. It is the ability to completely trust in what may not be tangible in the moment. Your first act of faith was asking Jesus to come into your heart. Unfortunately, without a faith-filled perspective the concept of victory will be one that is very difficult to grasp and obtain.

When it comes to the victorious life, our faith or trust must be found in God's promises. Sadly, many of us live a life where we have found faith in other things. Faith in our job security, parents, spouses, friends, talents, or our own abilities, either keep us afloat or leave us discouraged. At some point in life, these things will disappoint us. This is just the reality of life. People will leave your life. Jobs may downsize. And one day, your own ability and talents may not be good enough to get you to your goal. However, the great news is that when your faith is anchored in Christ, you can truly be secure, despite your circumstances.

I encourage you to dig into the verses below and meditate on what God says about His words and promises for you.

Numbers 23:19 - God is not human that he should lie; not a human being that he should change his mind. Does he speak and then not act? Does he promise and not fulfill?

2 Corinthians 1:20 - For no matter how many promises God has made, they are "Yes" in Christ. And so, through him the "Amen" is spoken by us to the glory of God.

Isaiah 55:11- So is my word that goes out from my mouth: It will not return to me empty, but will accomplish what I desire and achieve the purpose for which I sent it.

Let this sink in today! The truth speaking, life giving, everlasting, unstoppable, forever, loving, unexplainable, uncontainable, never ending God has promises for YOU! He cares about His promises to you, not because it's the right thing to do, but because He MUST! He's established from the beginning of time that He cannot and will not lie to you! If He says it, IT IS SO!

It is estimated that the Bible holds over 3,000 promises from God to you! Meditate on a few below in lieu of today's reflection verse. These verses of His promises will serve as the foundation for your perspective shift. They will counteract every moment of defeat, if you are willing to trade in your glasses!

He promises to strengthen you. Isaiah 41:10

He promises to save you. John 3:16

He promises to comfort you. Matthew 11:28, Psalm 147:3

He promises to never leave you. Deuteronomy 31:6, Joshua 1:5, 1Kings 8:57

He promises to heal you. Psalm 30:2

He promises to protect you. Psalm 23: 1-4, 2 Samuel 22:34

He promises to give you what you need. Philippians 4:19

He promises to give you a victory. John 16:33, 1

Corinthians 15:57, Deuteronomy 20:4

Reflection Questions

1.) Have you seen God's promises in your life? Reflect on a time that you saw God's goodness on your life.

2.) Have you found faith to be a difficult concept? What events in your life have discouraged or encouraged your ability to have faith in God?

3.) Name a few of God's promises that resonate in your heart. Which Bible verses reassure you of these promises?

Day Six

Lies and Truth

Before we go any further, we must address the elephant or sneaky snake in the room, the devil. It is important that we recognize that there is an enemy that will **attempt** to rob you of the victorious life God has ordained for you!

In fact, the Bible is clear; the enemy comes to steal, kill and destroy. It is his goal for you to live a life where you have no trust in God and where you believe the lies he tries to serve you.

I once said it like this, "The enemy can only offer you a serving of suggestion." As with any serving or dish, it is up to us take a spoon of the lies, spit it out, or refuse it altogether. Many are used to accepting the enemy's voice! We can literally have a belly full of lies from the devil. You can be so full of the enemy's lies that hearing anything opposite will simply not digest. However, we can also be so full of God's truth, that any lie from the enemy will literally not sit well in the pit of your stomach. In fact, you will find that when you encounter one of enemy's lies over you, you will literally be disgusted. Today, I offer you the opportunity to reject the plate of lies and dig into the buffet of truth that the Lord wants to offer.

Distinguishing the truth from a lie can be difficult. I have heard it said like this, "The enemy's voice, your voice, and God's voice can sound exactly the same in your head." Recognizing the difference will be essential in your journey of victory. There is a simple way to decipher the origin of your thoughts. Any thought that attempts to rob you of your joy, depress you, condemn you, make you feel "less than" or discourage you is not from God. God does not seek to tear you down, but to always lift you up.

Or as I like to say it, "If it isn't holy, it isn't from the Holy Spirit."

The enemy, on the other hand, has an entirely different tactic. He likes to inject your thought life with doubt. This doubt can range from doubting who God is, to doubting that God can love a "person like you." He whispers thoughts of doubt, rejection, fear, hopelessness, and depression. Your enemy is so ruthless that he will even use those closest to you to hurt you with words. In many cases, you will find that you can become so accustomed to his lies that you believe these things are "just who you are" or "just what you deal with." But the truth of it all is that there is no lie that the enemy can speak that can override God's love for you.

God's words over you will always reflect His love. His love for you was evident before you even spoke a word, or had your first breath. In fact, He decided long ago that you were worth dying for. Let me repeat that so it can sink in. The Creator, the Everlasting One, The Perfect One, decided that YOU were worth dying for. The Bible says He has more thoughts of you than the grains of sand. He even knows how many hairs are on your head. Take a moment and choose a small patch of hair, and start counting. You can be assured, that it would be quite impossible. However, God says He knows you down to the very thoughts you think.

This brings us back to the truths versus the lies. Why would a God who loves you so dearly whisper to you things that would break you down? Why would a God who desires to be so intimate with you speak words of depression, defeat, or hopelessness over you? What does He gain from harming the one He loves so dearly, which is you?

We must begin to discern between God's truth and the enemy's lies. Here are a few examples of thoughts that the enemy has attempted to trip me up with over the years.

You will never be good enough.

What is so special about you that people would care about you?

Life would be easier for everyone if you weren't around.

You will never reach that goal.

Things always go bad for you.

See, God doesn't even love you.

You are just a scary person, and that keeps you safe.

With that in mind, consider these words **God** has spoken over me.

You are good enough.

You will never be called insignificant again.

I have placed beautiful treasures inside of you.

I have called you to be a loyal friend that many can trust.

I will bless you to be the mother of nations.

I will use you to prophecy over others.

You will be used to proclaim the victory of God to the nations.

When you compare these phrases, it can be very easy to distinguish how the enemy speaks and how God speaks. God's words will speak hope. God's words will speak love. God's words will speak victory over your life.

Whether you are new in Christ or have been a

Christian for years, I challenge you to consider if you have been taking in more lies or truth. I challenge you today to pray for clarity in recognizing what truths and lies have been spoken to you over the years. Remember the enemy is well aware that YOU ARE VICTORIOUS! The moment you accepted Christ, you won! The only thing the enemy can do is convince you that you are not worthy or confuse you about who the Lord is! I pray that you no longer are a victim of this tactic from the enemy.

Reflection Verse

John 10:10- The thief comes only to steal, kill, and destroy. But I have come that you may have life, and have it to the full.

Reflection Questions

1.) When thinking over your life, what lies have been spoken to you from the enemy? Which ones have you accepted and allowed to become a "part of your identity" over the years?

2.) What words have God spoken over you? (If you aren't sure, refer to the list of promises found on Day 5) Have you accepted these?

3.) What action steps can you take to reject the lies of the enemy? (Prayer, reading God's word, etc.)

Day Seven

Going Deep with Christ

Before we go any further, we must address your relationship with Christ. This will be the key to your success. Maybe you accepted Christ for "fire insurance" as a child. Or maybe your idea of God is one that is distant, cold, or untouchable. I can assure you these are thoughts I could relate to years ago. I spent years asking how could there be a God. Who created this God? I spent years questioning a God who I did not quite understand. However, I find that the more I accept a relationship with Him, the more my faith arises. I am able to see past those things, and I am still learning to understand and allow Him to speak to me.

Honestly, His love has been evident in so many moments of my life that it would be foolish to deny His existence. He has transformed me from a fearful, timid, fatherless, depressed and broken girl, to a woman who has been delivered from so many different forms of bondage and relies fully on Him. I have many examples of how the Lord touched my heart, healed me, protected me, transformed my marriage, and answered prayers that I had not even uttered out loud. This is not because I am special or because God loves me more than others. It is simply because I have chosen to say "yes." I have chosen to accept His love as my guiding source and to seek Him at all times.

The key to going deep with Christ will come in your time with Him. God is seeking the ones who will speak to Him, who will come to Him for comfort, and who will love on Him despite the circumstance. Have you ever been in a relationship with someone who didn't speak to you? Have you ever loved someone who did not express to you their heart for you? It can be very difficult. Now, the great news is that God knows every thought. This means that there is nothing you can say to Him that will catch him off guard. However, much like the person who never speaks in a relationship, it's only a matter of time before the relationship grows distant and stale. It is only a matter of time before things, people, and distractions will turn your eyes away from the relationship.

The truth is God wants to constantly be on your mind. Just like the mother who loves to hear her child say the word "mama", the Lord yearns to hear from you. He loves it when we pray to Him. Whether it's a silent prayer, a loud cry, a song of worship, or even a moment of shouting your pain to Him, God wants you to speak to Him like you would speak to your best friend. He wants you to speak to Him like a father and one you can trust.

Going deep with Christ is a daily decision. This decision will cost you something. It will cost you not looking at what is happening around you. Instead, your focus will need to be on Christ and how He can be fully glorified despite the situation. Consider this metaphor below.

Imagine Jesus leading you. Literally, leading you. Grabbing you by the hand, and moving at a pace that you know you must keep up. Suddenly, you get to the ocean and He dives in holding your hand. As you go deeper and deeper into the ocean, you start to feel the pressure of the water. Your ears start to feel the clogged sensation. You want to feel anxious, but there's no time because you are heading deeper and deeper. You are going into areas of the ocean that you never thought you should go. Fully immersed, out of your environment, uncomfortable, yet.... following. In fact, you want to follow. You NEED to follow.

You know that where Jesus is leading you will be good. It will be life changing. You can't help but to feel safe. You have chosen to follow Jesus into the deep. Where others may have turned and swam to the surface, you keep following. No matter what, you make up your mind. I WILL go where He leads me. No fear. No shame. No hesitation.

When you stop to ponder who God is, your mind must shift from how far am I willing to go, to where wouldn't I go?

The question today is, are you willing to go deep with

Jesus? Are you ready to seek Him even when you think it may be uncomfortable or a situation you have never encountered? I once heard it said like this, "If you only want a splash, that will be available to you. However, if you want to be fully soaked in His presence, that is available as well." I choose to go all the way with Christ. Quite frankly, I've tried it the other way, and it simply did not work. Let this week be the start of going deeper with Christ. Set a time each day to give to the Lord. Whether 10 minutes or 45, every moment counts. This time may have to be creatively planned, such as on your way to work, or after your children are asleep. Don't worry, God will see your heart and meet you right there. Use a great daily devotional, a Bible app, or ask God to give you a specific area of the Bible to dig into. Your relationship with Christ and how serious you take going all the way in with Him will be instrumental for walking out the victorious life that He has for you.

Reflection Verse

Jeremiah 33:3- "Call to me and I will answer you and tell you great and unsearchable things you do not know."

Reflection Questions

1.) How would you describe your relationship with Christ?

2.) Are there areas of your life that you would be nervous to go deep with God?

3.) What are some ways you can go deeper with God in your life? (journaling, joining a church, etc.)

PART 2

Victory Blockers

Day Eight

Victory Blockers

It can be impossible to truly walk in victory when you are carrying around years of baggage.

Unfortunately, sometimes our biggest enemy is "IN-A-ME."

In other words, our own actions may be blocking us from having a life that is victorious! The victorious life is one that is hopeful, prosperous, purposeful, joyful, and confident in the future. This life is one that we should have as children of God. Remember, He desires for us to have life, and have it abundantly (John 10:10).

Obviously, in life we cannot control all things. This section is not about feeling guilty for going through life or having baggage. However, if you are honest and examine your life, you may find that you are missing out on your best life, simply because you have chosen not to let it go. Here are just a few victory blockers to consider. Be honest with yourself and evaluate if any of these are present in your life today.

1.) Lack of Integrity
2.) Pettiness
3.) Comparison
4.) Disorganization
5.) Shame
6.) Lack of Prayer
7.) Blaming
8.) Pessimism
9.) Isolation
10.) Dishonesty
11.) Gossip
12.) Jealousy
13.) Unforgiveness
14.) Sarcasm
15.) Rage
16.) Toxic Friendships
17.) Fear
18.) Bad Habits
19.) Dishonoring Authority
20.) Holding onto Past Hurts
21.) Being Easily Offended
22.) Impure Motives
23.) Lust/Fornication
24.) Pride
25.) Disobedience

What would your life look like if you removed any of these from your routine?

The reality is, this list can be daunting and leave us

feeling defeated. This is especially true when these areas have stuck around so long that we believe they have become a part of our "personality." The great news is that you DON'T have to continue to carry around these things. I once heard baggage considered as hooks.

While we think we are carrying our baggage, it is actually carrying US!

Imagine each of these items above as individual hooks in your side! Even allowing two of these areas to hook into your body will make you drag, tire quickly, and be drained! NOW imagine if you are carrying five or ten! Friends, we have to let them go. If you are unsure where to start, think to yourself, "one hook at a time."

Here's the thing about hooks in your side. Things WILL get messy, bloody, and uncomfortable, when you try to remove them. Nonetheless, once you get rid of the extra weight of these victory blockers, you will be freer to run into your destiny!

This is true freedom! I love the Bible verse that says....

Psalm 55:22 - Cast your cares on the Lord and He will sustain you; He will never let the righteous be shaken.

Imagine if you had to carry 150 pounds for a mile and someone offered to help! Would you say, "no, I want to feel the burn"? Probably NOT! You would tell them "yes"! That's the amazing thing about God. He says, I will take those things that you have been holding onto and allow you to be free. They never were intended to be a part of who you are or a part of your character. You must allow God's attributes to define you...like being patient, kind, loving, not envious, not boastful, not proud, not easily angered, and keeping no record of wrongs. Be a person who always desires to protect, always trust, always hopes and always perseveres! (I Cor 13:4-7). Allow God's words to develop your true identity, not the victory blockers above.

With God on your side, those things that have blocked your victory can truly be a thing of the past. All YOU have to do is be willing to LET IT GO!

Pray today that God begins to remove those hooks out of your life! Ask Him to show you the root of your actions. Ask Him for the truth about who you are and who He has called you to be. If you don't know where to start, say this simple prayer.

Heavenly Father. I repent of _____. I ask that you show me the lies I have believed and remove this thing that has been dragging me down. I ask that you teach me how to let it go, and change what has been harming me. Help me trust in you during this process. I lay this down before you so that I can live a life of victory and hope. Forgive me for allowing _____ to have authority over my life. Thank you Lord for helping me step out of this issue and into a greater version of me! In Jesus name, Amen!

Over the next few days, we will be exploring common victory blockers, what the Bible says about them, and pray specifically concerning them. Please know that removing anything from your life is a process; it may not happen overnight. Instead, it will take intentionality, a separation from the old things, and having an attentive ear to the Holy Spirit. Ask the Lord to send others who can keep you accountable and pray with you over these issues.

Reflection Verse

Romans 3:23- For all have sinned and fall short of the glory of God.

Reflection Questions

1.) At the moment, what would you consider your top three victory blockers? (Even if they are not listed above) Can you trace the root or where it all began? (Rejection from childhood, betrayal, etc.)

2.)) How have you found these things affecting your everyday life or those around you?

3.) What advice would you give to someone else carrying around "extra baggage"?

Shame and Guilt

Shame and guilt concerning your past are major victory blockers. Many of us have things that we have been through and experienced that we are not proud of. Some things are directly because of our own choices. Others, however, are not our fault. There are times when we are simply victims of unfortunate circumstance. Those who have been abused in childhood, raped, or betrayed may find themselves in a whirlwind of shame and guilt for these situations. This can be especially true if there is no way to confront the person who has done the offense.

In areas where there has been no sense of closure, we find ourselves in a cycle of continual self-blaming and shame for what has occurred. Likewise, for those who have done things previously on their own accord, there can be a huge amount of shame and guilt for your errors. I can recall inviting a girl to church months ago. She began to tell me how she was not very religious and felt ashamed to even enter the church. She truly believed her previous actions made her unworthy to enter the church.

She believed her choices had made her incapable of receiving the love of the Lord. For her, she was too "dirty" to enter a place deemed holy. There was a sense of humiliation associated with going to church. For her, it was easier to avoid the church, than to go in and risk being confronted for the person she believed she was.

The issue with the young lady is that she believed what she had done was synonymous with who she was. In other words, she allowed her actions to place an invisible stamp on her head. She allowed herself to carry the labels of her past. Many of us are carrying the labels of "molested", "reject", "single mother", "fatherless", "poor", "worthless "negative", "divorced", "addict", "whore", "cheater", "depressed" or so much more. These labels become the forefront of our existence. Thus, you are constantly stamped with the idea and label "not good enough." Not good enough for relationships. Not good enough for good things to happen to us. Not good enough to experience God's love for us. Not good enough for anything to go right in life.

Much like the hook metaphor discussed earlier in this section, these labels must be removed one by one. You must come to realize that the enemy loves to use shame and guilt as a tactic against you. The enemy recognizes if he can continue to frustrate and remind you of the past, he can have complete control over your future actions. The truth is we all have a past that we are not so proud of. I have learned your past will either empower your success or set the tone for your demise. We must use the past as a way to teach us. We must use the past as a way to look back and reflect. We must use the past as a way to encourage others. We must use the past as a way to draw closer to God. We must use the former shame as a reminder that God still forgives and God still loves us.

Isaiah 54:4- "Do not be afraid; you will not be put to shame. Do not fear disgrace; you will not be humiliated. You will forget the shame of your youth and remember no more the reproach of your widowhood."

Romans 10:13-For "everyone who calls on the name of the Lord will be saved."

Micah 7:19- You will again have compassion on us; you will tread our sins underfoot and hurl all our iniquities into the depths of the sea.

The Lord recognizes that we have all sinned. He recognizes that we are all in need of a Savior. Yet, He loves us through it all. The Lord does not come to condemn us or point the finger. When we mess up, He wants us to draw closer so that He can minister to us His unfailing love. He does not desire for us to run away. The Lord is not out to get us, or taking notes of all our horrible deeds. Instead, His goal is to give us grace and to love us beyond what man ever could. This grace and love does not give us permission to sin. Instead, He meets us where we are and seeks to heal our heart. He desires for us to move forward, and to not allow shame to cloud our judgement .

Dear Lord,

I ask that you open my eyes to areas where shame has taken over. Help me to cast every burden, every regret, and every fear unto you. Thank you Lord that you care for me and you love me beyond my mistakes and flaws. Forgive me for every time I have allowed shame and guilt to keep me from your love. Allow me to not be ashamed to share how you have transformed my life. Lord, every place that I have been carrying shame and guilt, I ask that you take it away now and show me how much you love me. Heal me in my broken places. In Jesus name. Amen.

Reflection Verse

Psalm 103:8-12 The Lord is compassionate and gracious, slow to anger, abounding in love. He will not always accuse, nor will he harbor his anger forever; he does not treat us as our sins deserve or repay us according to our iniquities. For as high as the heavens are above the earth, so great is his love for those who fear him; as far as the east is from the west, so far has he removed our transgressions from us.

Reflection Questions

1.) Is there anything in your life that you are ashamed of?

2.) How has shame or guilt affected your choices in life?

3.) Seek two Bible verses that speak on God's love and write them below. How does knowing God's love for you change your perspective on your past, present and future?

Day Ten

Leaving the Past Behind

In Genesis 17, God announces himself as El Shaddai. Shortly after, He changes Abram's name to Abraham and Sarai's name to Sarah. This leads us to ask why? Why would God declare himself El Shaddai, all powerful, before renaming them? The reality is that only the creator of a thing has the power to change its name and/or rename it. Each person that is renamed in the Bible is given a new destiny and identity. Their old name or previous associations are no longer who they are.

In the same way, who you have been in the past, is not who you have to continue to be. The old names, the old ways, the past regrets, past shame, can be eliminated and you can be refreshed with a new identity.

2 Corinthians 5:17- Therefore, if anyone is in Christ, the new creation has come: The old has gone, the new is here!

In other words, the moment you accepted Christ, He saw you as a brand-new creation. He stamped you with a brand-new name, "My beloved." The new creation you have become no longer has to be wrapped in the shame and guilt of the past. Instead, El Shaddai can transform you and remind you of who He has always seen you to be.

Many times, it can be difficult to escape your past. In fact, the world can make it nearly impossible to truly be set free. We can always count on those who have known us to remind us of who we used to be. This is further aggravated if you have to live with the proof of the past daily. For example, a person with a felony on their record has a constant reminder when they are looking for a job that they are a "felon." A woman who once dealt with drugs, will always be seen as a "recovering addict." Because society places labels on us, we must be intentional about moving forward. When you no longer recognize yourself as being entwined with your old way of life, you will gain strength to reject every label and word that says otherwise.

Truthfully, accepting a new name from God and letting go of the past is an issue of the heart. Some have been so wounded, so torn down, and defeated that their past seems like the only logical way to be. Their past has become their current expectation so much so that they willingly hold onto the past as a defense mechanism. If you have ever heard a person say, "All men are dogs" or "I expect things to fall through for me", then you can understand. These types of words confirm that the past has now set the tone for their present and eventually their future.

How can you live a victorious life if you aren't willing to move forward?

I love how the Bible says that all things work together for our good. The great news is that your past can work for you as it has taught you things. Your former ways should be a guide and a compass of what to steer clear from moving forward. There can be great value when examining brokenness and learning from it. With the proper perspective, your broken moments can become an encourager of your future strength. I encourage you today to review your life's story. Examine what areas of your past that you have been holding onto.

Reflection Verse

Isaiah 43:18 "Forget the former things; do not dwell on the past."

Reflection Questions

1.) What are some names or labels you have been given over the course of your life?

2.) Reflect on blessings you may have missed because of the disappointments of your past?

3.) Name some aspects of your new identity in Christ you will embrace the most? (Kindness, patience, etc.)

Day Eleven

Death by Comparison

Comparison can be seen as taking a knife and stabbing your own self in the back. In today's media driven society, it can be easy to compare your life with the neighbor, co-worker and celebrity who seem perfectly polished. For years, as a stay at home mother, I found myself doing the same. I would see many mothers selling products, getting fit, or creating clothes for their kids, and think I HAVE to do the same. There was an internal need to keep up. Although there was nothing negative about earning extra money, I wasn't living up to what the Lord had asked me to do in that season. Instead, my focus was to keep up with those around me who appeared to have the "perfect life."

Sadly, with each thought of comparison you are digging the knife deeper into your own back. The more your eyes are focused on those around you, the further away you are from being "true you." The more you give in to comparison, the more you betray your God-given, heaven-appointed, destiny. The reality is God has called you to have special abilities, talents, and values that are uniquely yours. Consider the following verses that shed light on God's plans for you and the trap of comparison.

*Jeremiah 29:11-For I know the plans I have for **you**," declares the LORD, "plans to prosper you and not to harm you, plans to give you hope and a future."*

*Proverbs 3:5-6- Trust in the **Lord with all your heart** and **lean not** on your own understanding; in all your ways submit to him, and **he** will make your paths straight.*

*Galatians 6:4-5 Each one should test **their own** actions. Then they can take pride in themselves alone, **without comparing** themselves to someone else, for each one should carry their own load.*

*James 3:16 For where you have **envy** and selfish ambition, there you find **disorder** and every evil practice.*

*Proverbs 14:30 A heart at peace gives life to the body, but **envy rots** the bones.*

These verses make it clear that He has plans for you. Additionally, it must be recognized that comparison is directly connected to jealousy. Jealously and seeking to have what others have is not only dangerous, but deadly to you. Your emotional health can literally ride on your ability to move past comparison. Furthermore, your spiritual health will suffer vastly.

Before moving forward, consider this example. Imagine having three children that you gave gifts to based on their personality, desires, and dreams. You gave a science kit to the child who has a love for experiments. Another child received a drawing kit, as he wants to be an artist. And the third received a baking kit, as this child likes measurements and creativity. As the parent, there would be an excitement and thrill that comes from watching your children come alive with their gifts. However, what would your perspective be if the child with the science kit became envious of the child with the art set? Now the child that has the gift of science is suddenly having sleepless nights over the art set that he did not receive. The reality is that as a parent you would want your children to trust that you gave them the correct gift and that you had their best interest in mind. In the same way, God has given you unique treasures that are for you to grab a hold of. I challenge you to LET GO of all areas of where you give into comparison and accept God's truth about who you are in this season of your life.

Truthfully, you will be unable to walk into your new life of victory hoping to have someone else's gifts and calling. God's plan of victory for your life requires you to say "yes" to all God has called for **you** to be. You will never walk in your true identity when you are jealous of another's.

Lord, I ask that you reveal areas where I have allowed comparison, jealousy, and envy take root. I recognize that I have dishonored you in not valuing the gifts you have placed in me. Help me to fully walk out your plan for me with no element of strife. I ask that you release me from the bondage of trying to be like others. Instead, help me to only imitate you in all my ways. It is my desire to trust you for the plan of my life. Open my eyes to see clearly what you have for me and how to walk in victory.

Reflection Verse

Psalm 138:8a-The LORD will work out his plans for my life–for your faithful love, O LORD, endures forever.

Reflection Questions

1.) Who are people in your life that you often compare yourself to? Why?

2.) When you consider your own life, what do you believe God has called you to do?

3.) Do you believe you have kept your eyes more on others' lives or the Lord and His plans for you?

Day Twelve

The Fear Trap

As a person who spent years in fear, I can assure you that fear will keep you from moving into the victorious life. Remember, victory means to overcome despite the opposition. Fear, however, places you in a constant state of opposition. Our fear is based on a perceived danger physically, emotionally, mentally, or spiritually. In many situations, the thing we are fearing may never come into fruition. Thus, fear acts as a barrier between you and what you are needing to move towards in life.

A common theme in our society is the notion of healthy fear. Many believe that fear is what "keeps them safe." Many argue that without fear we would make careless choices. Many argue that healthy fear is instinctual and needed for survival. Those who are proponents of this idea will often use the example of a child touching a stove. According to them, the healthy fear of getting burnt again turns the child away from the desire to touch the stove. Let's consider how fear is mentioned in the Bible.

Joshua 1:9-Have I not commanded you? Be strong and courageous. Do not be afraid; do not be discouraged, for the Lord your God will be with you wherever you go.

Isaiah 41:13-For I am the Lord your God who takes hold of your right hand and says to you, do not fear; I will help you.

God is making it pretty clear that He is not desiring you to be fearful. With that in mind, why would God desire for us to have any form of fear. In what scenario would fear deem itself "healthy"? Instead of healthy fear, let's consider the word caution. One who is cautious is aware of danger. Danger is a real aspect of everyday life. Danger can be seen in terms of "if-then" statements.

If I overdose on drugs, then I will be severely hurt.

If I drink and drive, then I can die.

If I don't stretch before I work out, then I may hurt myself.

You can make choices based on previous knowledge taught directly or indirectly. For example, you use caution in the kitchen, while cooking. You are aware that the stove can burn you. However, you have full control over the situation. Chances are you do not slowly creep up to the stove in fear. Instead you are aware, the stove is hot and you respect that fact or there will be consequences. Wisdom tells you not to put your hand in the flame. Fear tells you to be afraid of the stove and the flame.

As a Christian, you have an extra added tool, the Holy Spirit. The Holy Spirit is your personal protection that indwells within every believer. The Holy Spirit is that gentle small voice that says, "be careful" or "don't do this." You may have experienced in your own life driving and suddenly feeling a small voice telling you to go into another direction. I have heard countless stories of people who later learned that they had avoided a major accident by taking a different route. The Holy Spirit will give you divine insight and wisdom on choices to make to keep you safe. However, we will get into the gift of wisdom later in the book.

As a person who spent a large portion of her life fearful, OF EVERYTHING...I can tell you that FEAR is not something you can allow in your life at all. The fearful person is tormented by the "what if's." The person who exercises caution or wisdom is empowered by understanding. A wise person can hear what the Holy Spirit is telling them about the situation. A fearful person is too clouded by their thoughts, racing heartbeat, and panic to know what to do next.

Fear allows the unknown to lead. Wisdom allows the Holy Spirit to lead.

I encourage you to evaluate if you are living a life of fear or faith. The person of faith doesn't have to be fearful because they KNOW that God is with them. Fear will keep you from enjoying your life to the fullest. Fear will keep you in bondage.

Fear goes beyond being afraid of spiders, snakes and mice. Fear includes fear of failure, fear of lack, fear of disappointing others, fear of death, fear of being alone and so on. If you find yourself constantly being plagued by "what-if's," there is a high chance you are falling into the enemy's trap of fear. He knows that if he can keep you fearful, he can keep you isolated and unable to walk out your destiny. Make a choice to choose faith over fear!

Remember, the only fear you will ever find to be acceptable in the Bible is the reverent fear of the Lord. This is not a paralyzing fear, but a deep respect that seeks to honor Him. If your fear doesn't fall into this category, as most fears do not, it's time to let it go!

Recognize that the Bible describes fear as a spirit. The spirit of fear loves to attach to you and cause havoc in your life. However, you can get free from a life that is filled with fear. It will take a recognition that you no longer want this to be present in your life. Later in the text, we will go more into your authority over the various ways the enemy tries to attack you. Until then, ask the Lord to take fear from your midst in the prayer below.

Dear Lord,

Forgive me for allowing fear to be my guide. Help me to trust in you for my life. I recognize that fear is a spirit. I break fear from over my life. Spirit of fear you are no longer allowed to rule me and my choices. Go in Jesus name! You are no longer welcome in my life. Father, teach me to trust in you. Fill every space in my heart and mind where fear has tried to attack me with more of your love and peace. Thank you Lord for illuminating every area of my life I have allowed fear to take over me. Teach me how to listen closely to the Holy Spirit to guide me in wisdom. Amen

Reflection Verse

2 Timothy 1:7 For the Spirit God gave us does not make us timid, but gives us power, love and self-discipline.

Reflection Questions

1.) What are some fears you struggle with? (Failure, death, certain animals, etc.)

2.) Write on a time in your life when fear caused you to miss an opportunity?

3.) In an ideal world, how would you describe the fearless version of you? What things would you do that you normally would be hesitant about?

Day Thirteen

Getting Rid of Toxins

A recent documentary stated the following, "Just because something is less toxic, doesn't make it not toxic."

In other words, toxic is toxic. Unhealthy things are unhealthy. Foolish things are foolish. Many times, we attempt to rationalize our behaviors and thought patterns with the notion of comparison. The alcoholic will say "At least, I'm not addicted to heroin." The womanizer will say, "Well, at least I don't physically abuse my ladies." The glutton will say, "Well, at least my eating habits only affect me." Whatever, the case it can always be easy to minimize our actions. Minimizing allows us to believe that our actions "aren't so bad". Truthfully, if there was a scale of negativity some things would rank higher. However, negative is negative.

This brings us back to the concept of toxins. Toxins are not meant to do you well. Occasionally, there are some things that are toxic that can be useful in very small doses or when used appropriately. For example, cleaning solutions can work miracles for a dirty kitchen but are not intended for digestion. In general, things that are toxic stunt your growth, have a negative impact, and act as a poison in your life. These are areas of your life that you can truthfully live without.

In my own life, one area that I have felt convicted about is watching certain reality shows that are full of cursing, fighting, fornication, and rage. After watching such shows, I could see myself behaving like the women in the show. Picking up their phrases, responding like they do, or even having a "ready to fight" attitude, became a part of who I was. Although I could see how these shows were toxic for me, I literally could not get enough of them. I would rationalize, "Well, this is just my guilty pleasure." It almost became my badge of honor when witnessing to others. It would be like a "Hey, guys I'm not perfect I like dirty television." In some cases, I would watch these shows just to have something to talk about with my friends who also loved it. While in other circumstances, these shows reminded me that my life just "isn't that bad." Whatever the case, I could always give a very rational excuse for why I needed to watch fighting housewives, super bad girls, and the most outrageous hip hop stars. Despite all my excuses, every time I watched, the Lord would stir up a conviction and speak, "You are better than this." Slowly, I began to wean myself of this area that was acting as my personal poison.

If you are honest, what are the toxic areas in your life?

The urge to gossip?

A friend that must be let go?

An addiction that is ruining your life?

A distraction that is hindering you?

A sin that you commit often?

The list can go on and on. Consider the following verses concerning allowing toxins in your life. I believe this will help open your eyes to those things that you participate in that are toxic.

Romans 12:2-Do not conform to the pattern of this world, but be transformed by the renewing of your mind. Then you will be able to test and approve what God's will is— his good, pleasing and perfect will.

1 John 2:15 Do not love the world or anything in the world. If anyone loves the world, love for the Father is not in them

Colossians 3:5 -Put to death, therefore, whatever belongs to your earthly nature: sexual immorality, impurity, lust, evil desires and greed, which is idolatry.

James 3:10- Out of the same mouth come praise and cursing. My brothers and sisters, this should not be.

Mark 7:20-23- He went on: "What comes out of a person is what defiles them. For it is from within, out of a person's heart, that evil thoughts come—sexual immorality, theft, murder, adultery, greed, malice, deceit, lewdness, envy, slander, arrogance and folly. All these evils come from inside and defile a person."

Ephesians 4:26-27- "In your anger do not sin": Do not let the sun go down while you are still angry, and do not give the devil a foothold.

Acts 3:19- Repent, then, and turn to God, so that your sins may be wiped out, that times of refreshing may come from the Lord.

1 Corinthians 15:33- Do not be misled: "Bad company corrupts good character."

These verses make it clear that there are plenty of toxic things we can allow. From cursing to adultery to arrogance, we have to be very intentional about moving forward without the toxic waste. The victorious life is one that is difficult to attain when you are carrying toxins that are all around you. Imagine a person who literally was carrying 10 pounds of foul toxic waste over their shoulder. The reality is that this person would be repulsive. They would literally carry a stench that would make people not want to be around them, promote them, or draw close to them. This can directly affect your ability to be victorious. Furthermore, how can you walk in a life of full victory when you choose actions that cause a direct separation from the Lord. I urge you to consider the areas of your life that require a complete overhaul. Allow the Lord to give you a spiritual cleanse from the toxic waste.

Dear Lord,

I ask that you forgive me for allowing _____ to overtake my actions. I recognize that _____ has hindered me and my relationship with you. I ask that you remove my desire to _____ and that you replace it with the urge to live a life is upright and pure in your sight. Teach me your ways Lord and allow me to walk fully in your promises and your plan for my life. Help me to have discernment on the things in my life that are acting as a poison to me. Send people that can help me to be accountable and can pray with me in these areas. In Jesus name. Amen.

Reflection Verse

James 4:17- If anyone, then, knows the good they ought to do and doesn't do it, it is sin for them.

Reflection Questions

1.) Name some behaviors or relationships that you indulge in that are toxic.

2.) What would be the benefits of no longer doing these actions? Are you ready to give them up or are there some that you refuse to let of at the moment? Why or why not?

3.) What Bible verse above spoke to you the most concerning toxins you may be dealing with?

Bitterness

Unforgiveness is the poison that keeps giving. For many of us we have justifiable reasons we have chosen not to forgive. Deep betrayal, abuse, deception, and more can lead us unwilling to forgive. We often think, "Well, you don't know what they did to me." Please know that God is fully aware of the circumstances that have taken place. In my life, I have found instances where I have withheld forgiveness. There was an aspect that believed, "If I forgive them, they will continue to mistreat me." However, forgiveness is not a hall pass to allow others to mistreat you. Forgivingness is the ability to accept what has happened and choose to move forward with the Lord's help. It is not for the offender, but for you!

Matthew 18:21- Then Peter came to Jesus and asked, "Lord, how many times shall I forgive my brother or sister who sins against me? Up to seven times?" Jesus answered, "I tell you, not seven times, but seventy-seven times"

Here are a few reasons why we must forgive from a

biblical standpoint.

1.) We forgive because Jesus forgave.

Luke 23:3a- Jesus said, "Father, forgive them, for they do not know what they are doing."

Ephesians 5:1-2- Follow God's example, therefore, as dearly loved children and walk in the way of love, just as Christ loved us and gave himself up for us as a fragrant offering and sacrifice to God.

2.) We forgive so that we can be forgiven.

Mark 11:25-"And when you stand praying, if you hold anything against anyone, forgive them, so that your Father in heaven may forgive you your sins."

Matthew 6:12 -And forgive us our debts as we also have forgiven our debtors

3.) We forgive so that we don't become bitter.

Ephesians 4:31-32- Get rid of all bitterness, rage and anger, brawling and slander, along with every form of malice. [32] Be kind and compassionate to one another, forgiving each other, just as in Christ God forgave you.

The Bible makes it abundantly clear that forgiveness is necessary. Forgiveness is our way of telling God that we will trust in Him for our healing. I once heard it said like this, "Not choosing to forgive is like exalting yourself higher than God." In other words, if God, the most perfect one, can forgive the liar, the murderer, and the corrupt, how can we choose to not forgive? We must recognize that we must forgive so that God can forgive us. The Lord forgave us for living a life that was unworthy. He forgave us for the times we have walked away and betrayed him in idolatry and more. How then, can we not give the same honor to those around us? This is not always an easy process, but it is necessary.

How can you be victorious when you have those in your midst that you hate? How can you be victorious when you are bitter about their actions towards you? Victory places your eyes on Christ. Unforgiveness places your eyes on those around you. I have found the following to be strategies for how to forgive those who have harmed me.

1.) Recognize your own sin.

Matthew 7:3- "Why do you look at the speck of sawdust in your brother's eye and pay no attention to the plank in your own eye?"

2.) Let go! Let God handle them and you.

1 Peter 5:7- Cast all your anxiety on him because he cares for you.

3.) Allow time for God to heal you.

Psalm 147:3 He heals the brokenhearted and binds up their wounds

4.) Pray for those who have offended and yourself.

Philippians 4:6- Do not be anxious about anything, but in every situation, by prayer and petition, with thanksgiving, present your requests to God

Some wounds are too deep to just say "I forgive you." Just like in your physical body, many deep wounds will take time to heal. Some wounds may even leave a permanent scarring. This is the case for situation of extreme betrayal or abuse. Never forget that your scars will never diminish who you are. Instead, your scars are a cry of victory for the world to see. Your scars remind you that if I survived this, I can survive the next thing. Forgiving others is not a license for allowing individuals to continue to scar you. Instead you can say, "Although you have wronged me, I will move forward in victory." I will move forward knowing that every plan meant to hurt me can be used for God to bless me. When you start to view life through the eyes of love and forgiveness even the worst moments can be ones that remind you of God's faithfulness.

Forgiveness will be instrumental in your journey towards victory. Unforgiveness will allow you to continue to drink of the waters of bitterness. You cannot afford any poison in the life that God has created for you. I challenge you to no longer allow bitterness and unforgiveness to demolish your victory walk. Over the next few days, truly pray that the Lord allows you to break free from all those whose actions have kept you in a spiritual bondage.

Reflection Verse

Colossians 3:23- Whatever you do, work at it with all your heart, as working for the Lord, not for human masters.

Reflection Questions

1.) Write a list of those who you have not forgiven and an abbreviated aspect of what they did to you? (Example- Mark-Betrayal) Think as far back in your past as you can remember. After doing so, call them each by name and ask the Lord to remove all forgivingness towards them from your heart. If you feel led and it is appropriate, pray about reaching out to certain individuals and telling them that you forgive them!

(Another idea is to do this on a separate sheet of paper, pray to forgive each person, and tear up the paper as a sign of letting go!)

2.) Do you believe that God calls us to forgive and forget? What have you learned from your past hurts with people?

3.) What are some things that you have resisted being a part of due to bitterness and unforgiveness? Missed opportunities? Leeriness of future relationships?

PART 3

Walking Out Your Victory!

Day Fifteen

Every Day Victory

A lifestyle of everyday victory is one that we can all have. In the previous days, we have discussed the attitude of victory, the foundation, and common victory blockers. However, the last 6 days we will go into a few core principles of how to walk in victory!

Let's consider what has been discussed thus far are the first steps in your victorious life.

Your Relationship with Christ- Your relationship with Christ will be the key to your success. Maybe you accepted Christ for "fire insurance." However, I encourage you to re-examine your relationship. Assess how you can build an even stronger relationship with Him! The stronger your connection, the easier it will be to hear His voice. This will be vital to know how to navigate your steps. The Lord desires for you to draw near to Him and live out the plans He has for you! Ask the Lord for wisdom on how to strengthen your connection.

Your Faith - 1 John 5:4 says we will achieve victory through our faith. In other words, it will be our faith that takes us from being defeated to being victorious. Your faith in God will always speak the opposite of what your physical eyes can see. If your doctor says you have one month to live, your faith will declare, "I shall live and not die" (Psalm 118:17). If your teenager is going astray, your faith will declare "My child will not depart from you Lord" (Proverbs 22:6). Your faith will encourage you when all seems to be going astray. A faith-driven perspective will allow you to remain aware that God is always looking to bring you out of every battle. This perspective will allow you to bounce back from every difficulty being stronger than ever.

Fighting the Real Enemy - Many of us fail to walk in victory because we are unaware who the real enemy is. Your neighbor or co-worker may act pure evil, but they are NOT the real enemy. The devil is the one who seeks to "kill, steal, and destroy" (John 10:10). He will use every weapon against you. Slander, gossip, temptation, fear, rejection are just a few of his tools. And he has NO issue using those you love to make it happen. The enemy hates relationships. We see this with Adam and Eve. He knows if he can turn you against each other, he has won. Instead, let's fight the real enemy. Even Jesus experienced the enemy's attempts. But with every try, Jesus fought the enemy with the Word of God (Matthew 4:11). REFUSE to accept any thought that attempts to rob you of your victory. Recognize that if a thought defeats you, shames you, or causes you to not move into what God has called you to do, it is NOT from God!

Victory Blockers- Recognize the things in your life that are blocking your victory. Often times, we can be very busy blaming others for why we are stagnant. However, there are many things we allow to stay present in our life that are acting as road blocks in our own victory. The enemy loves to keep us in bondage through fear, shame, bitterness, offense and more. Take time to truly look over the list of victory blockers listed within the book. These may single handedly sabotaging you! The great news is that there is NOTHING that is too difficult for God to handle. Every area of your life that the enemy is attempting to block you, the Lord can restore you and deliver you from!

Remember, the enemy is well aware that YOU ARE VICTORIOUS! The moment you accepted Christ, you won! The only thing the enemy can do is lie to you to convince you that you are not worthy or confuse you about who the Lord is! Over the next few days, I believe you will be equipped with the ability to see through the lies and recognize all the more that God has a great plan in store for you!

Reflection Verse-

2 Corinthians 10:4-5- The weapons we fight with are not the weapons of the world. On the contrary, they have divine power to demolish strongholds. ⁵ We demolish arguments and every pretension that sets itself up against the knowledge of God, and we take captive every thought to make it obedient to Christ.

Reflection Questions

1.) Over the last few days, what areas have you been challenged in concerning victory?

2.) What areas do you find the enemy attacks you the most? (Fear, envy, strife, fornication)?

3.) What steps have you or can you start to take to move forward in your life from these everyday issues?

Day Sixteen

The Lifestyle of Prayer

In the world of Christianity, many often toss around the phrases "I'm praying for you" or "I will pray about that." The reality is that this is just common jargon for many and there are few prayers truly occurring. If this has been your way in the past, it can no longer be the case. A lifestyle of prayer will be essential for you to walk in the complete victory that the Lord desires for you to have. Prayer is literally the key to it all. In fact, although you could apply several principles of the book to have a "better life", it won't help you to truly have an inside-out change.

The truth is that the day you accepted Christ into your life, His victory on the cross laid the foundation for you. His resurrection was the proclamation that you had the ability to tap into all that the Lord has promised for you. It gave you the authority to fight against the devices of the enemy. It gave you the ability to tell every demon and every weapon formed against you to flee in Jesus name.

In other words, if you never did another thing in this life your very acceptance of Christ gave you full access to the throne of God and the benefits associated. This is not because of who you are or your power, but by the power of the Lord! This is victory!

Nonetheless, many Christians will find themselves constantly defeated, overwhelmed, and easily distracted by the enemy's devices. I believe this is because they have not tapped into the power of prayer. Prayer is the supernatural key that unlocks heavens blessings onto Earth. Prayer is your two way communication between God and you to cause change in your life and the world around you. Prayer is your reminder to the Lord that you will seek Him first for all that you need.

This intimate conversation between you and the Lord will be where you find your direction and where He will make very clear the path that He wants you to take. It's difficult to know the ways of a person that you do not foster relationship with. In the same way, prayer strengthens your relationship with Christ and helps you to know His ways and know His voice in your life. This will allow you to properly make choices in your life and towards your calling. This will keep you from going down paths that lead to your demise and shift you into the direction where the Lord is looking to bless you the most.

As a mother of five, with one on the way, I can relate to the many who think "This is great, but I have no time to pray." I can assure you that many of us are full of time, we just are unaware. The time you devote to your favorite television shows could be prayer time. The time you spend driving to work could be prayer time. The time you spend quietly reading a book could be prayer time. The time you spend arguing with a friend or spouse could be prayer time. Time is all around you. If you are honest with yourself, you can find that there are many times in your day that you can dedicate to God. This will look differently for each person. For a mother of five, this time may come in the early morning before her children awakes. For the business man, this time may come during a lunch break. For the commuter, this time may come while on the way to work. Whatever the time you choose, make it intentional and make it devoted to the Lord. Of course, distractions will come on occasion. However, it is vital that you devote your energy into fitting in these moments.

Years ago, I read a book that talked about "whisper prayers." These prayers are those that you quietly say under your breath. They could be as simple as "Lord, help me" or "Speak to me Lord." But these kinds of prayers, keep God in the forefront of every situation. In essence, your entire life can be built around prayer and communication with God. If you are feeling frustrated at work, you can pray "Lord, help me." If a friend seeks your advice you can pray, "Speak to me now Lord." In other words, your default setting can always prayer. Your very life can be a constant flow of prayer. Much like the person who cannot help but to curse in any moment of aggravation, you can learn to pray in the same manner. The Bible makes it plain that prayer and seeking the Lord is a vital aspect of the Christian walk.

2 Chronicles 7:14- if my people, who are called by my name, shall humble themselves, and pray, and seek my face, and turn from their wicked ways; then will I hear from heaven, and will forgive their sin, and will heal their land.

Ephesians 6:18- And pray in the Spirit on all occasions with all kinds of prayers and requests. With this in mind, be alert and always keep on praying for all the Lord's people.

Romans 12:12 - Be joyful in hope, patient in affliction, faithful in prayer

Never forget that prayer is not just a way to give your list of wants to God. It is also for praying for your family, enemies, your country, and the world. It is your way to hear God's direction and strategy for your life. It is also our way to ask for forgiveness and seek help in our everyday issues. We see that even Jesus recognized the importance of prayer, often drawing away from the crowd to pray to the Father. Today, you must decide if you are willing to go even deeper with Christ and pray relentlessly. Will you allow prayer to be your guiding force and your default setting? If so, walking out a life of victory will come with ease as you will be directly connected with Him!

Reflection Verse

Matthew 6:9-13- This, then, is how you should pray: 'Our Father in heaven, hallowed be your name, your kingdom come, your will be done, on earth as it is in heaven. Give us today our daily bread. And forgive us our debts, as we also have forgiven our debtors. And lead us not into temptation, abut deliver us from the evil one.'

Reflection Questions

1.) What sticks out to you about the content of this prayer model given by Jesus?

2.) What do you find you pray about the most? (finances, anxiety, your dreams, etc....)

3.) Name times that you can set aside to pray daily.

Word Power

Battle- a hostile encounter or engagement between opposing forces

Illness, job loss, the disobedient child, marriage woes, or financial difficulties are not battles we love to endure. In fact, they are quite overwhelming to experience. These experiences rock us to our core and make us question why! The truth is your weapon in EVERY battle will be the Word of God!

His words will speak peace to your chaos. They will speak victory to your battle. When you learn how to pray God's word over your life, you will find you no longer have to run from battles. Instead, you can move forward with great strength in knowing that if God be for you who can be against you! The promises that you find in the Bible are for these moments to give you hope in a hopeless situation!

Although your first response to adversity may be to

isolate, be depressed, or wallow in self-pity, you MUST fight the devil with the Word of God! We see this model even with Jesus in the following passage.

Matthew 4:8-11-Again, the devil took him to a very high mountain and showed him all the kingdoms of the world and their splendor. "All this I will give you," he said, "if you will bow down and worship me." Jesus said to him, "Away from me, Satan! For it is written: 'Worship the Lord your God, and serve him only.' Then the devil left him, and angels came and attended him.

Allow your words to be His words when facing the enemy. There are some of us that have even become accustomed to using words to even sabotage ourselves. The Bible says that the power of life and death in the tongue. In other words, you can literally shape the world around you by your declarations. As a child of Christ, there is great authority that can come from your mouth! We see this from the beginning of time when God spoke. He said, "Let there be" AND there was! In the same way, your words have creative power. The question is what things are you declaring out loud. Are you declaring that you are "broke", "will never make it", or "are not good enough"? If so, do yourself a favor and STOP! We must use our words to hinder the enemy not destroy our own selves. Consider this approach instead.

When you are faced with a disease, **DECLARE** "by your stripes I am healed! (Isaiah 53:5)

Lose your job, **DECLARE** that the Lord will provide for his children (Psalm 37:25)

The enemy trying to convince you that you are not loved, **DECLARE** God loves me (John 3:16)

Feeling afraid**, SPEAK** peace over your life and mind (2 Timothy 1:7)

No matter what the battle, we do NOT have to run away with our tail between our legs! God has given us power to speak over our situations with great authority! This is a privilege of being created in the image of the Creator! The depth of the battle is irrelevant. If you are following the Lord's leading, His words will always place you in a winning position! Don't stop fighting! Don't stop using God's words to declare victory in every situation.

Reflection Verse

Proverbs 18:21-The tongue has the power of life and death, and those who love it will eat its fruit

Reflection Questions

1.) Do you speak more words of life/victory or death and defeat over your life?

2.) What words have been spoken over your life can now you recognize are not from the Lord?

3.) List areas of your life that the enemy has come to speak death over you! Find Bible verses that speak the opposite of this and write them down beside each lie of the enemy.

Day Eighteen

The Gift of Wisdom

(By Joseph Riollano)

Wisdom- the soundness of an action or decision with regard to the application of experience, knowledge, and good judgment.

Another way to define wisdom is the ability to take a situation and make a good logical choice based on the factors of the situation. It is important to recognize that the Bible speaks of worldly wisdom and the wisdom of God. Worldly wisdom is based on what you can see and interpret based on your own knowledge. Godly wisdom is directed by the Holy Spirit and supersedes the experiential or book knowledge that you may currently have.

1 Corinthians 1:30, "It is because of him that you are in Christ Jesus, who has become for us wisdom from God— that is, our righteousness, holiness and redemption."

According to the above verse, the Bible looks at wisdom and says that wisdom is Jesus. For context purposes, read 1 Corinthians 1:18-31. In this passage

Paul was talking to the Corinthian church and explaining to them that the message of Jesus dying on the cross was a crazy concept for unbelievers to accept. For nonbelievers, the message of the cross doesn't appear to be a very trustworthy story or wise to believe. However, if you are a Christian, then you know that it's very unwise NOT to believe Jesus died on the cross. In fact, the core of your faith is resting on this fact. Either way, we see that many moments in life are about deciding between worldly wisdom and Godly wisdom. Accepting the message of the cross itself is a clear picture of the distinction between God's wisdom and human wisdom.

I challenge you to think about the entire Bible. Remember all the stories and verses that you can.

Does the Bible tell us to trust ourselves or to trust Jesus?

The answer is, the Bible always encourages us to trust in Jesus. Although many things in life can appear to be a result of choices, wisdom is different. The Bible describes Godly wisdom as a gift. This gift is one that now empowers you to make choices that are good, with proper timing, and that reflect the heart of God.

James 3:17-18 "But the wisdom that comes from heaven is first of all pure; then peace-loving, considerate, submissive, full of mercy and good fruit, impartial and sincere. Peacemakers who sow in peace reap a harvest of righteousness."

I believe that these verses are a key to truly living and

understanding what Godly wisdom really is. Here you see that James says that wisdom is pure, peace-loving, considerate, submissive, full of mercy and good fruit, impartial and sincere. If wisdom has to do with human ability, then as a human it would be impossible to live up to these verses' outlook on wisdom. As humans, we do not always display these characteristics at all times. Now this is a good time to thank Jesus for His grace and mercy!

These verses are really talking about the character of a person. Think about it, the first verse we read told us that Jesus is God's wisdom. If you know Jesus, you know that Jesus had the qualities listed in the James 3 verses above. When thinking about wisdom as qualities instead of choices or decisions, then your very character should include wisdom. The great news is that if you are a Christian, the Holy Spirit will give and be the wisdom you need for every choice you are faced with.

As you walk out your victorious life, remember the seven qualities that wisdom consist of.

1.) Purity, honesty and openness
2.) Peace-loving, showing kindness
3.) Considerate
4.) Submissive, respecting authority
5.) Full of mercy, and good fruit, forgiving
6.) Impartial, showing no favoritism
7.) Genuine

If you don't have these qualities or you feel like you need help in any of these areas ask the Lord to give them to you, *"If any of you lacks wisdom, you should ask God, who gives generously to all without finding fault, and it will be given to you" (James 1:5).*

It is important to recognize that we MUST ask the Lord for Godly wisdom. We can never attain too much Godly wisdom. Wisdom will give you discernment with people, your calling, timing of choices, and so much more. Wisdom is a gift that is necessary for all who want to live a life that opposes the enemy and desire to walk victory! Praise the Lord that this gift is available to anyone willing to ask.

Reflection Verse

Proverbs 4:6-7-Do not forsake wisdom, and she will protect you; love her, and she will watch over you. The beginning of wisdom is this: Get wisdom. Though it cost all, you have get understanding.

Reflection Questions

1.) According to the seven qualities of wisdom, what areas do you struggle with?

2.) What are other verses you can find on wisdom?

3.) Do you find that you operate in your own wisdom or Godly wisdom more?

Day Nineteen

The Inner Circle

As a military wife, the word "squad" is often heard in my community. A squad is defined as a small group of people organized in a common endeavor or activity. This term is most often used in the sense of a tactical military group. Your squad is that inner circle that you can count on to fight alongside. Your squad should help to speak life into your passionate purpose.

My friends, who's in your squad?

Is your squad full of those you can trust to get you through tough times?

Is your squad full of those who encourage you to do better?

Is your squad helping or hindering you?

Does your squad gossip, quarrel, compete, and envy?

Does your squad encourage, uplift, and help carry you in prayer when you are in battle?

Your squad is important. They will play an essential role in how you get through your battles. You squad is your inner circle of friends. Some say we are the average of our friends. In other words, if I never met you, a close look at 2-3 of your closest friends will reflect who you are.

Your inner circle can make or break your victory!!

Consider the soldier on the battle field. In the heat of a war, where so many are falling around him, he's not looking for a wimpy team. In fact, he's looking for those who can carry him off the battle field. Those who can see the enemy, when he can't see the enemy. Those who can encourage him when he's ready to run away from the fight. Those who won't put him down when things didn't go according to plan.

His squad must be strong.

His squad must be merciful.

His squad must have his best interest in mind.

There will be no time for nonsense on the battlefield. He will need the others, and they will need him. Can you imagine if the soldier had to deal with a different kind of squad? A squad that was so full of jealousy for him maybe they didn't rescue him when he needed it? A squad who only looked out for themselves on the field? A squad who criticized every move he made on the field? A squad who was so busy talking about other squads they were distracted? Our soldier, would be in a terrible situation if this were his squad.

It's time to assess your squad. Will your squad be perfect? No, we live in a world of imperfect people. Will there be those in your inner circle who are not as strong as you spiritually or emotionally? You bet! But, we can all make choices for who we allow in our inner circle. Unfortunately, everyone cannot be in your inner circle.

This group of people that you hold close to you must be chosen wisely. Remember VICTORY is not subtle. We are ALWAYS in a battle spiritually. Recall, the enemy of your soul is constantly seeking to kill, steal and destroy you! He has no plans to take it easy on you and will wage war on you at any given moment! The question is who can trust to take into battle with you? Who can you count on when you are in the darkest moments of your life?

In order to walk victoriously, you may need to reevaluate those who you have allowed to influence your choices. The goal is not to start cutting off your childhood friends. The goal is to surround yourself with those who can encourage, who can pray for you, who can filter their advice for you through the word of God. Ultimately, the closer you are to Christ the more He will illuminate those around you that you need to draw close to. In addition, He will make it clear when a relationship requires a separation and shift. Pray that the Lord continuously keeps your eyes alert to how you can foster friendships that glorify Him.

Reflection verse

1 Corinthians 15:33- Do not be misled: "Bad company corrupts good character."

Reflection Questions

1.) Who are some friends that add value to your life? What makes them different?

2.) If you are honest with yourself, are you a good squad member to others? In what ways do you add to the victory in other's lives?

3.) Write a list of those in your current squad. What characteristics do you find in each of them that benefits the group?

Day Twenty

Integrity Counts

Integrity- being honest and having strong moral principles; moral uprightness. Being whole and undivided, consistency

Proverbs 20:7 The righteous lead blameless lives; blessed are their children after them

Luke 6:31- Do to others as you would have them do to you.

2 Corinthians 7:2 - Make room for us in your hearts. We have wronged no one, we have corrupted no one, we have exploited no one.

In today's society, the concept of integrity is not something that is taught. In previous generations, we could hear people speak phrases like "Your word is everything" or "Your word is a bond." We see that many around us can be flaky or only be honorable to the extent that it benefits them. However, a life of integrity encourages you to be honest, trustworthy, consistent, and always seeking to "do the right thing". Although many aspects of having a victorious life will be spiritual, we cannot overlook the practical things that may be hindering you. You must truly ask yourself if are you a person of integrity. This will require a tough look at yourself in the mirror. Consider the following statements.

Are you dependable?

Do you treat people well solely for selfish reasons?

Are you time conscious?

Do you honor confidentiality amongst your friends?

Can others trust you?

Do you do the right thing when no one's looking (this goes from putting back the grocery cart to turning in a missing wallet)?

Do you value others?

Do you keep your word to others?

If you answered no to one or more of these questions you may struggle with integrity. Integrity will affect our ability to walk into what God has called for. Perhaps you may be denied certain blessings due to your lack of this basic principle. For instance, why would your boss promote you if you are always late? Why would your friend entrust you with being a business partner, if they are unable to trust you with a secret? Why would you be asked to do a long-term job, if you are not loyal?

Although God can surely bypass these flaws, it is essential that you recognize your part of the deal. It is plausible that the Lord may allow you to work on these things before walking in your promotion. If not, you may self-sabotage your destiny. The Lord is so good that He will protect you from YOU! He will work with you on maturity while you are on the way to living out your destiny. Your ability to show integrity, initiative, and maturity will be essential for walking out the victorious life.

Reflection Verse

Proverbs 19:1- Better the poor whose walk is blameless, than a fool whose lips are perverse

Reflection Questions

1.) Tell of a time that you showed integrity and another where you did not show integrity.

2.) What aspects of integrity do you struggle with?

3.) Integrity means whole and undivided. Do you find that you are whole and undivided in your walk with Christ and values?

Day Twenty-One

Embracing the Father's Love

The final day is dedicated to you recognizing how much God loves you! The reality is that if you cannot accept God's love for you, you will find it difficult to believed that you are worthy of a great life! Regardless of what you think God thinks of you, His love for you is unstoppable. So much that He believed you were worth dying for! As a woman who's lived a life of being betrayed, full of shame, fatherless, depressed, fearful, I can understand why some have a difficult time connecting with the Father's love. At one point, I truly believed I was downright unlovable.

His eyes towards you are blazing with an intensity, a fire, an unquenchable passion. Formed from the beginning of the Earth, His love sees right pass all insecurities, doubts, fears. THIS love reaches your past and stamps it VOID! This love sees you pass what you could ever see yourself. It's quite frankly boundless. The Father's love for you outweighs every negative word spoken over you. The Father's love breaks every chain that has kept you. The Father's love makes what you thought was impossible, possible. Indescribable. Never ending. Passionate. Never Failing. All for you. All for me.

You see, when I came to know God's love, EVERYTHING CHANGED! The shame, the guilt, the insecurities, the confusion, and the lies of the enemy, began to fall off one by one. I came to recognize that I do not serve a cold and distant God. Instead, I serve one who is very personal. I began to understand that He has a great plan for me! His plans are for me to be prosperous, victorious, and live a life that shows His goodness!

2 Chronicles 16:9a- For the eyes of the Lord range throughout the earth to strengthen those whose hearts are fully committed to him.

Embracing the Father's love for you is essential. This is what will empower you to move in your passionate purpose, to live a life of integrity, to seek a connection with Him, and to rid yourself of victory blockers! When you recognize how much He loves you, you will have an inner fire to walk out your purpose and to not look back. Remember the Father's love goes far beyond what your eyes can see or the labels others have placed on you. Instead, it says from the beginning of the Earth, He called you HIS and stamped you with victory! Pray the following prayer aloud!

Dear Lord,

Thank you for being the love of my life. Thank you loving me when I have been unable to love myself. Lord, I recognize you as the Creator of the Universe and lover of my soul. I ask that you remove the areas of my heart where I have allowed myself to feel unlovable. Fill my empty places with a new revelation of your love and who you have called me to be. Help me to walk in your full plans of my life. I ask that you encounter me through dreams, visions, and your people and speak your plans of victory and hope over my life. Thank you, Father, for surrounding me with your love. In Jesus name, amen!

Reflection Verses

Romans 8:37-39-No, in all these things we are more than conquerors through Him who loved us. For I am convinced that neither death nor life, neither angels nor demons, neither the present nor the future, nor any powers, neither height nor depth, nor anything else in all creation, will be able to separate us from the love of God that is in Christ Jesus our Lord.

Reflection Questions

1.) Do you find it difficult to embrace God's love? Why or why not?

2.) What would it look like for you to recognize God's love and plan for your life? What would you do differently?

3.) Does knowing that the Creator of the Universe loves you make you feel empowered to make changes in your life, perspective and relationship with Him? What will you do next to walk out this life?

Conclusion

Congratulations, you have started the first steps towards living a life of complete victory! Truthfully, it would take a yearlong devotional to truly tap into all God says about victory! Regardless, the goal of this book was to shift your perspective on having a victorious life. Additionally, the hope was that you would consider the areas of your life where you have allowed defeat to override your thoughts and actions. Please note that although you may have followed along with the prayers and ideas presented, you may still have moments of defeat. Be aware that the enemy will be attempting to hit you on every side. He literally cannot stand the idea of you tapping into God's promises. This is not the time to cower; this is the time to fight the devil with the Word of God. This is the time to pray even more. Feel free to use the verses and prayers in the book to refresh what you have learned in the book!

Remember the defeated life was never for you! Once you accepted Christ into your life, you signed up for a life that could be full of greatness! However, the Lord is looking for you to take steps. Every step counts in victory! Transitioning from a defeated mindset to a victorious one will be a transition process. It will take intimacy with Christ and seeking His wisdom on your actions. Transitions may not be pretty, but they are necessary. You will find that the more you fill your life with His words for you, the more you will experience a life of victory everywhere you go!

Here are a few final tips to continue walking on the path of victory from this day forward.

1.) Find a community that supports and encourages you. A local church or Bible study is a great resource!

2.) Set a time aside daily to pray and listen to what the Lord is saying. Make this time intentional and a priority.

3.) Purchase sticky notes that you can write Bible verses on! Place them around your home as a reminder.

4.) Guard your eyes and ears! If you find that something you are indulging in draws you away from God. Let it go!

5.) Keep a journal of your thoughts and prayers.

6.) Ask the Lord for wisdom overall and in daily choices.

7.) Forgive all those who have wronged you! Do not forget to forgive yourself.

8.) Remember if your thoughts are speaking love, hope, or positive direction, they are from God. Resist all other thoughts!

9.) Maintain a winning attitude! Never forget the pro-wrestler example! God has pre-determined that the battle is rigged in your favor! If you fall get back up! No matter the outcome, as a child of Christ...you WIN!

10.) Take authority over your tongue! Line your words up to God's words! The power of life and death are in your tongue.

11.) Remember who the REAL enemy is! Your battles are fought spiritually through your usage of the word of God and your faith! Your victory rides on this principle.

12.) If you have not accepted Christ, wait no longer! Ask Him into your heart today! Your life depends on it!

May you continue to walk a life of complete victory in every area! May His face shine upon you and His words be the heartbeat of your soul! Go forth victorious one in the path He has for you! Take your victory steps boldly, knowing that His love will carry you every step of the way!

Victory Verses

John 3:16- For God so loved the world that He gave His one and only Son, that whoever believes in him shall not perish but have eternal life.

Deuteronomy 20:4- For the LORD your God is the one who goes with you to fight for you against your enemies to give you victory.

Matthew 11:28 "Come to me, all you who are weary and burdened, and I will give you rest."

Romans 12:2- Do not conform to the pattern of this world, but be transformed by the renewing of your mind. Then you will be able to test and approve what God's will is—His good, pleasing and perfect will

Numbers 23:19- God is not human, that he should lie, not a human being, that He should change his mind. Does He speak and then not act? Does he promise and not fulfill?

John 10:10- The thief comes only to steal, kill, and destroy. But I have come that you may have life, and have it to the full.

Jeremiah 33:3- Call to me and I will answer you and tell you great and unsearchable things you do not know.'

Romans 3:23- For all have sinned and fall short of the glory of God

Psalm 103:8-12- The Lord is compassionate and gracious, slow to anger, abounding in love. He will not always accuse, nor will he harbor his anger forever; he does not treat us as our sins deserve or repay us according to our iniquities. For as high as the heavens are above the earth, so great is his love for those who fear him; as far as the east is from the west, so far has he removed our transgressions from us.

Isaiah 43:18- Remember not the former things, nor consider the things of old.

Psalm 138:8- The LORD will work out his plans for my life–for your faithful love, O LORD, endures forever. Don't abandon me, for you made me.

 2 Timothy 1:7 For the Spirit God gave us does not make us timid, but gives us power, love and self-discipline.

James 4:17- If anyone, then, knows the good they ought to do and doesn't do it, it is sin for them.

Colossians 3:23- Whatever you do, work at it with all your heart, as working for the Lord, not for human masters

2 Corinthians 10:4-5- The weapons we fight with are not the weapons of the world. On the contrary, they have divine power to demolish strongholds. We demolish arguments and every pretension that sets itself up against the knowledge of God, and we take captive every thought to make it obedient to Christ.

Matthew 6:9-13- This, then, is how you should pray: 'Our Father in heaven, hallowed be your name, your kingdom come, your will be done, on earth as it is in heaven. Give us today our daily bread. And forgive us our debts, as we also have forgiven our debtors. And lead us not into temptation, abut deliver us from the evil one.

Proverbs 18:21- The tongue has the power of life and death, and those who love it will eat its fruit.

James 1:2-4-Consider it pure joy, my brothers and sisters, whenever you face trials of many kinds, because you know that the testing of your faith produces perseverance. Let perseverance finish its work so that you may be mature and complete, not lacking anything.

1 Corinthians 15:33- Do not be misled: "Bad company corrupts good character.

Proverbs 19:1 Better the poor whose walk is blameless than a fool whose lips are perverse.

Proverbs 4:6-7-Do not forsake wisdom, and she will protect you; love her, and she will watch over you. The beginning of wisdom is this: Get wisdom. Though it cost all, you have get understanding.

Romans 8:37-39- No, in all these things we are more than conquerors through Him who loved us. For I am convinced that neither death nor life, neither angels nor demons, neither the present nor the future, nor any powers, neither height nor depth, nor anything else in all creation, will be able to separate us from the love of God that is in Christ Jesus our Lord.

Ephesians 6:10-18-Finally, be strong in the Lord and in his mighty power. Put on the full armor of God, so that you can take your stand against the devil's schemes. For our struggle is not against flesh and blood, but against the rulers, against the authorities, against the powers of this dark world and against the spiritual forces of evil in the heavenly realms. Therefore put on the full armor of God, so that when the day of evil comes, you may be able to stand your ground, and after you have done everything, to stand. Stand firm then, with the belt of truth buckled around your waist, with the breastplate of righteousness in place, and with your feet fitted with the readiness that comes from the gospel of peace. In addition to all this, take up the shield of faith, with which you can extinguish all the flaming arrows of the evil one. Take the helmet of salvation and the sword of the Spirit, which is the word of God. And pray in the Spirit on all occasions with all kinds of prayers and requests. With this in mind, be alert and always keep on praying for all the Lord's people.

ABOUT THE AUTHOR

Victoria Riollano is a military wife, mother of six and lover of the Lord. She is married to Joseph Riollano, a true servant and minister of the Lord. Victoria holds a Bachelor's Degree in Child and Developmental Psychology and a Master's Degree in Psychology. Currently, she works as a Psychology professor and is the founder of the Victory Speaks blog! Victoria's written works have also been featured on several noted sites such as Encouraged in Heart, Daughters of the Deep, and the She31 Network.

She serves in various areas of ministry including worship, youth, speaking, administration and social media. Her goal is that every person she encounters experiences the love of Christ. She believes that God's desire is for believers to walk in true victory! The defeated life that is lonely, confused, and lackluster is not for those who know who they are in Christ. Victoria is proud to proclaim that God has delivered her from depression, promiscuity, suicidal thoughts, fear, and so much more. Victoria believes that through the wisdom of the Holy Spirit she can inspire many to wake up and recognize their true identity in Christ.

Made in the USA
Columbia, SC
03 July 2020